TREASURE GIVEN ON BROKEN PATHS

TREASURE GIVEN ON BROKEN PATHS

Life's Difficult Paths are Strewn
with Exquisite Treasure

DEBORAH LEWIS

XULON PRESS

Xulon Press
555 Winderley Pl, Suite 225
Maitland, FL 32751
407.339.4217
www.xulonpress.com

Unless otherwise indicated, Scripture quotations taken from the New King James Version (NKJV). Copyright © 1982 by Thomas Nelson, Inc. Used by permission. All rights reserved.

Paperback ISBN-13: 979-8-86850-077-0
Ebook ISBN-13: 979-8-86850-078-7

Endorsements

When you are looking for wisdom and guidance through very painful seasons, you and I would most likely turn to those who have traveled these same difficult journeys and have come through them with a healthy and life-giving perspective. Deborah Lewis has provided just that for all of us, who have gone or will eventually go through such a season. Treasure Given on Broken Paths offers wisdom, hope, and the profound love and presence of God to those who will face struggles or disappointment in life.

Jerry Sweat

There is something in your story that God is going to take and use in the form of multiplication. He is about to multiply your reach.

Doug Snead

Deborah's book will be a beaten down, shaken together, bearing much fruit book. Deborah and Dean are my Old Way favorite friends. The Old Way is looking at the unseen realm. It is not heaven; it is the very heart of God. Not just angels, but God's very heart.

Connor Perez

This Holy Spirit inspired book is going to open hearts and eyes and reopen hearts and reopen eyes that have been shut for a very long time. This Holy Spirit inspired book is going to save many lives as they read how loved they are by God. It is going to put a smile on a face that has not smiled in a long time. It is going to put a tear in an eye that has not wept in a long time. It is going to refill a spot that has been empty. Most of all, it is going to bring healing to soul wounds. It's going to bring hope to the hopeless and a fire to ones who have never had a fire inside of them. This book is going to reach ones who are angry at God and the world; pastors, churches and their families. This book is going to inspire others to speak life over themselves and the people around them. It is going to help them realize how to forgive themselves of their past and their present through Christ.

David Lyons

About the Author

*D*eborah Lewis has twenty-four years of experience teaching students with special needs and varying exceptionalities. Currently, she works as a media specialist in a large urban school district. Deborah is a Veteran of the US Naval Reserve. Along with her professional career, she faced many personal challenges, including six and a half years of infertility, two seasons of helping raise other people's children, developing the discipline required to pay back every cent of tens of thousands of dollars of debt, a miscarriage, a crisis pregnancy with a daughter diagnosed with Trisomy 18, raising three beautiful daughters, one with special needs, the death of that daughter, and divorce.

Through these experiences, Deborah noted that God was always there, His presence and His hope. In the trying, painful times, He was depositing His treasure. This book is filled with the nuggets of truth that she collected along these broken paths. These are "cliff notes" to help you focus your heart and mind on your life's journey. May you be abundantly blessed in all your ways.

For I know the thoughts that I think toward you,
says the LORD, thoughts of peace and not of evil,
to give you a future and a hope.
(Jeremiah 29:11)

Dedication

I would like to dedicate this book to my amazing parents, Tom and Liz Neville. They taught their six children many important things, but most importantly, to love people and find joy in every situation. As extroverts, they threw fun parties, complete with sack races and balloon tosses every Fourth of July and Christmas parties where the kids would dress for the nativity play.

My dad would talk to complete strangers when we were out and about. He would place quarters in my hand in the pew at church so that I would have something to plop into the basket as it passed. Although he couldn't carry a tune in a bucket, he sang from his heart every Sunday morning.

My mom would prepare meals for people who were hurting and characteristically prepared thoughtful gifts on various occasions. She would stand in my doorway at night and lead the prayer for our family. She is still actively volunteering at her church in their outreaches to the homeless. She shares joy wherever she goes. She is ninety years young.

She watches over the ways of her household and does not eat the bread of idleness. Her children rise up and call her blessed: Her husband also, and he praises her.
(Proverbs 31:27-28)

Thank You

I would like to thank my daughters, Kathryn and Janae. You are visual reminders that God answers prayer. You are God's, "Yes," to over a decade of my pleas asking for children. I am so proud of the women you have become, abounding in equal amounts of inner and outer beauty. You are both focused and will find much success in your future endeavors. Kathryn, thank you for allowing the use of one of your childhood creations. Janae, keep sharing the gift of your beautiful voice. Thanks also to Dean, my husband, for his faithful care and support for me. Your technical skills have enhanced this project at every turn. Thank you to the Tuesday Night Girls and daily texting partners, Susan, Rose, and Roddy, and the many friends that helped me on difficult days and enthusiastically read my blogs and written offerings. I have such an amazing support system. I could not possibly name everyone that was a part of my broken but beautiful journey. Many have listened, caught tears, given words of encouragement, and told me hard truths even if I could not process what they were telling me at the time. I am truly blessed.

Along the way, my sister, Barbara Summers, has been a world class listener. Barbara, you encourage me to always do better in that area. Your skills were an agent of healing in my life. Thank you for the beautiful cover. Karen Bary, thank you for listening to the first drafts of my blogs and always encouraging me to keep at it. We have had so many fun adventures along the way, and our birthday video will be bringing joy for years to come! Thank you to Jennifer Snead, David Lyons, Penny Kennedy, and the Perez family for reading the draft of this book and offering great tips and wisdom. Thank you, Diane Fulp, for coming in during the fourth quarter of this project and sharing your editing skills. Thank you, Jim Moore for being a lifelong friend and contributing four photos to this effort.

I thank my God upon every remembrance of you.
(Philippians 1:3)

Table of Contents

List of Illustrations

Introduction

*T*hank you for taking the time to read bits and pieces of this book. When I came to know Jesus in a profound way at the age of fourteen, I thought that life would be easy. I was mistaken. My life was irrevocably transformed as the fundamental cry of my heart became, "What do You want, God?" instead of just going about my way, pleasing myself and other people. I have zero regrets about that decision, but I truly did not realize life was fraught with so many obstacles, trials, oppositions, and flat-out painful experiences. I thought if I loved God with my whole heart, I would be successful and happy. I have come to realize that happiness and joy are radically divergent substances.

These past few years have been profoundly challenging globally. No one was excused from loss(es) or perplexing tests. I wrote this book to help comfort, heal, and inspire you. My biggest takeaways on the bumpy roads are two-fold: Don't *ever* give up, and cling. Cling to the cross until you have splinters. Cling to God's promises until, like Joseph in the Bible, you distantly discern the footsteps proceeding the clanging of the keys. The day had come to free him of the constraints of the prison cell. His years of preparation were complete. In all ancient Egypt, he became second in command only answering to Pharoah. His years of training built a character that blessed the entire kingdom and surrounding lands. In the same manner, maybe your life is about to have a positive course alteration? Can you hear approaching footsteps? Can you imagine the hands that are readying and positioning the keys to open doors for you? Your future is bright.

So, read one thought, a chapter, or the entire volume. Let this book be utilized in your life in a way that makes sense. You are in the right place at the right time. You have a destiny, and it is my hope that you participate with God to reach it!

Get wisdom! Get Understanding! ... Do not forsake her, and she will preserve you.
(Proverbs 4:5-6)

Chapter 1

The Makings of a Treasure Hunter

$\mathcal{L}$ ittle girls love to play dress-up, Barbies, and house. They love to dance, skip, and run. Some are brought to church and taught to stay quiet, keeping busy by looking at religious books and children's Bibles. They are instructed to put quarters in the offering basket when it passes, having been given the coin only seconds before the required action. As part of their nighttime routine, they are taught to say bedtime prayers. I was a little girl of that sort. As the energetic mother of a bustling home,

I am sure it was not always timely for my mom to drop other activities and lead my sister, Elizabeth, and me in prayer. She would stand at the doorway to our room in a narrow, dimly lit hallway as we were already bathed and cozy in our beds. She would proceed with folded hands and reverently bow her head.

"God, bless Mommy, Daddy, Peggy, Tommy, Barbara, Patrick, Elizabeth, and Deborah. God, bless everyone. 'Our Father, Who art in Heaven, hallowed be Thy Name. Thy Kingdom come, Thy will be done on earth as it is in Heaven. Give us this day our daily bread, and forgive us our trespasses, as we forgive those who trespass against us; and lead us not into temptation but deliver us from evil. Amen."

She would leave the door slightly ajar allowing beams of dim light to dowse our room. I was afraid of the dark, much to the chagrin of my older and braver sister. This routine is the foundation of my prayer life.

In all those evenings, it never occurred to me to pray for strength or endurance. I had zero understanding why the prayer Jesus used as a model would include a need to forgive and ask for deliverance. In all my childhood experiences, I never needed God to rescue me. We were a happy bunch, well cared for, active, and full of wonder.

At the age of fourteen, my life was radically transformed at FCA (Fellowship of Christian Athletes) camp in Black Mountain, North Carolina. The keynote speaker must have been six feet, two inches tall and all around enormous, weighing close to 300 pounds. Her story was more compelling than her physique. She had been a prostitute, a madam. She had done many wild things in her former life, even mentoring others to follow her lead. She spoke of our Savior with a gentleness that was entirely disarming. This Son of God, bruised, broken, tortured, and murdered, loved her so thoroughly. She allowed Him to love her. In my imagination, I saw that she had been given a small box, intricately wrapped, as an eternal Christmas gift. She had opened it! The treasure within was Christ Himself! This in exchange for the life that she had lived in such complicated fleshly bondage. Then, she extended this same gift to us: the promise of eternal, purposeful life in exchange for all our misdeeds, all our self-centered teenage whimsical wishes.

An altar call was given. I froze like a deer in the headlights. How could I, who had lived my whole life trying to be a good person, take that step down the aisle in humility in front of everyone? How could I, raised Catholic, take that step out and up? I wrestled with myself. Stubbornly, I anchored myself, harboring safety in my established pride. I would not budge for the reckless, public involvement at that altar, up front where the girls were weeping, exchanging their sin for freedom. Nevertheless, His Word, through the speaker, had penetrated deeply. What happened in the anonymity of my wooden chair was nothing short of a life transformed. What had been a routine of waking up and trying to decide what I wanted would henceforth become a lifestyle of arising and consulting, "What do You want, Father?"

The verse, which served as the focus of the entire week, was James 1:2-4 (NIV): "Consider it pure joy, my brothers, whenever you face trials of many kinds, because you know the testing of your faith produces perseverance. Let perseverance finish its work, so that you may be mature and complete, not lacking anything." We were asked to memorize this scripture. With the exception of the Lord's Prayer, this was the first Bible verse I had ever memorized. In my naivety, I had no idea why the Bible would talk so much about pain and trials. I was an American from a healthy family, and my father was always providing for us and loving our mother. My perception of Christianity would continue to be filtered, for many years, through an Americanized lens of "everything will be good and happy," just like the ending of a Disney movie. Later in life, when I was thirty-nine and in the throes of a painful traumatic trial, these words would begin to be life-giving, a sort of oxygen mask, when all the chips were crumbling.

It started as a bright, sunny, Florida, day full of promise. My family of four packed into the blue Ford minivan. Our destination, the doctor's office. This was a special appointment for women who are consider high-risk due to the mother's age. As I had been a patient there several years earlier, for my pregnancy with Janae, our focus that day was the first sonogram and gender reveal of the baby!

One thing caught my attention as we sat waiting: The nurses and doctor celebrated in the hall. They were ecstatic; another patient's tests had come back negative. The staff was truly joyful. They jumped up and down with jubilation. Her baby would be fine. Unconsciously, I formulated a surprising musing: "I wonder if they will rejoice like that for me?"

We entered the exam room bringing a variety of laughter and curiosity. Janae, age four, with wavy brown hair and bright hazel eyes, was inquiring about all the equipment in the room. Kathryn, age nine, with her strong broad smile was her norm, full of life and exuberance. Sonogram goop was applied to my belly to facilitate the wand's mobility. It was a beautiful moment. I consciously took notice of the entire scene and hid it in my heart.

Once the technician announced, "It's a girl!" I focused on the screen. I noticed the baby's head didn't look quite right. I couldn't put my finger on it, but the shape looked off somehow. This did not remind me of Kathryn and Janae's sonograms. *How peculiar.* I asked the tech what she was doing. "Counting digits," was her reply. I proceeded to do the same. "One, two, three, four, five, six. Six!" My baby girl had six fingers. I held my breath. My heart skipped a beat.

Things were amiss. Serious things were wrong with my daughter. Dr. Green came in and started talking quickly about all the abnormalities he was seeing. "And here, in the heart, it looks like there's a problem. And her head, it's not shaped right, see? It's called a strawberry-shaped head. There is a lot of water on her brain, on both lobes. That is called hydrocephalus. That might go away in the coming months, but I can't know for sure. And if you notice here—" and he zoomed in on the baby's hand, "excluding the thumb, I think I counted five finger bones, not four. And if you notice . . ."

I couldn't keep up with all the medical information that he was divulging. My husband, returning from the restroom, realized that Kathryn and Janae were being bombarded by this information. He whisked them away so they would not be further traumatized about the awful news about their baby sister.

The baby was eventually diagnosed as having Trisomy 18, Edward's Syndrome. You may have never heard of this. The doctors explained that it is more common than childhood diabetes, occurring in one out of five thousand births. Of the children who are not aborted, 50 percent never make it to birth; 50 percent of them do not survive one or two months, and 90 percent of them die before their first birthdays.[1]

My world and faith were rocked to the core by these revelations. The doctors were merciless in explaining over and over that she would die. They used a phrase that should never be used and is an outright lie: "She is incompatible with life." In the daze of grief, I took the thousands of pieces of my shattered heart to my home bathroom, which doubled as my personal space for prayer. My intention that day was to leave the God I had loved for a quarter of a century. "How could this be my reality? How could You let this happen to me? All I have ever wanted to do is serve You since I was a teenager, and this is how You treat Your daughter? This is my reality?" The tears flowed from the depth of my soul. The pain of this trauma was almost unbearable. As much as I purposed in my heart to gather all my playthings from God's sandbox and move out of His territory, there was only one thing that frightened me more than staying with Him. That was the thought of facing all of this on my own.

I knew from spending over a decade in a church that taught predestination that God was not surprised by this turn of events. He already had a course of action and a destiny for this child. I would be a fool to leave God, the only One who could guide me through this labyrinth of pain and misfortune. My preoccupation with the pain morphed into resolution.

"Father, I'm going to catch You being good. I'm going to search for You like searching for precious gemstones. I'm going to record every good thing You do for my family. All things work for good. All things are *not* good, but good can be found in this trial. I'm going to concentrate on that. I'm going to find that good and remember to thank you for it!

Instead of 'Why me?' I say, 'Why not me? Why not me?' I must trade my weakness for Your strength. My kids, my husband, need me to make it. They need me to be strong and not fall apart. Nothing is impossible with You. Your Word is true. I have to be an example to my girls. Please, help us. Bless my family. Spare our baby. Let her live. Heal her. In Jesus's name, I pray. Amen."

This is the journey that taught me the value of becoming a treasure hunter when life does not make sense. This book is filled with little nuggets that I picked up on days that my circumstances were not creating for me a "happy" life. This is the *pure joy* that James spoke of. We need vision to see it. We need to on purpose search for, recognize, caress and celebrate the pure joy that is helping us to be mature and lack no good thing. I hope in sharing some of my treasure found on broken paths, you yourself will have eyes to see the good that God is doing for you!

The baby was named Carly Joy, and she lived an extraordinary seven and a half years. Every day of her life was marked with pure love and pure joy! My family was surrounded by a small army of prayer warriors and support of many kinds in her education and through supportive family and loving friends. I am forever grateful to have been entrusted with the entire life span of another human being. It is a high honor to be chosen as the mother of a special child.

The Beautiful Life of a Special Child

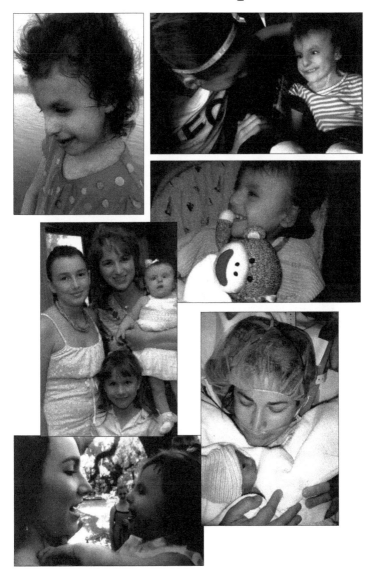

Chapter 2

Destiny

#1

I hope today you will find small wonders, simple joys, and a deep sense of self-acceptance. You are loved. You are powerful. You have a destiny. The One Who created you adores you. If you spend all your days apart from Him, He will still love you and long to give you the destiny He made for you. I'm not saying that destiny is easy, but it is powerful and can impact generations!

#2

Just because something is difficult, trying, or costly, doesn't mean that you aren't doing an amazing job! Chances are, you are! In the recesses of your mind, where most people never glimpse, always generate kind, gracious thoughts toward yourself. You are doing a great job!

#3

In the midst of your comings and goings, your obligations, and even your trials, do this: Enjoy your life! It's a unique gift that has only been given to you! Joy unspeakable and full of glory has been purchased for you! Claim your gift with the same fervor you use to shop or watch sports!

#4

Yesterday is over. Tomorrow is but a dream. Today is your moment. Be the best you that you can be!

#5

"When you consider everything you were born for, everything you have endured, and everything that you have encountered, know that I have equipped you and prepared you for this moment in time." [2]

#6

If your destiny includes doing anything of value, know that you will receive criticism, judgement, and opposition of many kinds. Don't worry. Focus forward. Your worth and value are priceless. You are someone worth dying for.

#7

Two of the most important things are who you are and where you are. More important still is where you are heading. You have gifts, talents, strengths, and weaknesses. You have one more thing: Destiny! Don't let anyone, anything, or any hurtful memory keep you from attaining that for which you were quite literally born. Be strong. Be courageous.

#8

What is your hope in? Politics? I have seen liars and cheats on both sides of the aisle. Medicine? I've seen people die of both COVID-19 and the shots. Money? You will take zero with you when your life ends.

My hope is in the One who has dried every one of my tears and provided every single one of my breaths. The Lord God Almighty is His name. When storms come, His name is a mighty tower. He sent His Son to love you back to your destiny. You are a dream come true from the Father's heart, but how can you fulfill that destiny apart from the One who created you? Believe in the Lord Jesus Christ and you will be more alive than you ever knew possible. He does not promise an easy life but one of profound purpose and eternal significance. Nothing you have done will disqualify you for Heaven. Nothing! He laid His life down to clear your way back to the Father. He knocks at every heart. Open that door. Let Him in.

#9

Sometimes you ask God for something very simple. Many difficulties ensue, but He answers by setting you free! (Think Moses asking for seven days to worship, and God releasing them from 400 years of slavery!) When that happens, allow Him to strip you of your slavery mentality and mantle you as a warrior. You are free! You are loved! Be strong! Be courageous! He fights for you. Step into your purpose and destiny!

#10

"The mountain and the memory of it will fade away and the promises, the DNA of your purpose will be revealed to you. The mountain will crumble, and you won't even have to walk on it, or get over it, because it is gone and God has removed it. Now He has your heart and now you know your purpose." [3]

Chapter 3

Perspective

#1

People will impose their bias on the story of your life. Cast it aside and toss it to the ground. Live your life. Live it with power and grace and tears, when necessary. You are one of God's gifts to this broken world. Shine! Shine! Shine!

#2

Walk your path with integrity, and you will have joy, without regret, even if you haven't found the exit to the furnace quite yet. Know that the future is bright. The best is yet to come. Hope is worth holding on to. You are loved, accepted, and provided for, to unfathomable depths. We are yet to touch, unpack, and utilize all that has been given for our benefit.

#3

Find something truly amazing about today and linger there. Fill your heart with simple and beautiful things.

#4

Resistance builds strength. Fight through opposition. You will come out with a few scrapes, bruises, and wounds, but you will now possess enhanced power, agility, and grit. When you win one battle, you get another battle. Your victories only increase.

#5

 I had never sat behind her grave. It was a beautiful view. These are some of the things you never grow up hoping for, but somewhere along the way, God decides this is part of your story, and with Him, you can handle it.

#6

If it takes more than two seconds to find something on your phone to show someone, their mind will typically wander. It does not speak well of our culture that we are professionally impatient. I am learning to be more patient, to give my full attention to the person standing right in front of me. I hope you are as well.

#7

In quiet moments, simply practice enjoying being alive. Every day is a gift. Enjoy your gift.

#8

I know we are at a gut-wrenching, tragic time in our nation. I know many are mad, sad, and grieving, all at the same time. I believe we will make it through, becoming better and stronger. I am sorry for all the pain that has surfaced. However, I know that pain acts as a homing device. It locates the precise places where healing needs to occur. In the darkness, light will shine.

#9

Don't look for life to get easy! It won't. Start looking for the beauty, friendships, and miracles that are sprouting along life's amazing pathways. The treasure is always there. Train your eyes to see it and your heart to savor it!

#10

So much about Carly's face was crooked, but she was stunningly beautiful. If more people had her love and joy, the world would be such a better place. For all the special children in the world, you guys rock! We need to learn from the lessons you teach.

#11

Keep the past in the past. Only visit previous negative occurrences to find freedom from their sting. The future is bright!

Chapter 4

Faith

#1

You are not a mistake, an inconvenience, or a disappointment. You are a dream come true from the Father's heart. He needs you here with all your strengths and weaknesses. Life is tough, sometimes brutal. He wants to heal, comfort, and restore. Here's the Great Exchange: all of what you hold in your hands for all of what He holds in His. "For unto us a child is born." (Isaiah 9:6)

#2

He loves you, because He loves you, because He loves you, because He loves you. That is Who He is. If He had wanted to hold anything against you, if He had wanted to punish you, He would not have allowed His Son to suffer so grotesquely. On the contrary, His desire is to throw all our sins away and simply lavish His love upon us, friend to friend.

#3

The feeling of confusion is just a way of explaining that the solution to a situation, task, or requirement simply hasn't come into focus yet. Confusion is just one step toward another victory. When you are confused, don't panic. Time and attention (wisdom and prayer) usually provide the needed "a-ha!" moment.

#4

When you consider the nearness in time and space of the cross to the empty tomb, never be afraid to assess the hurts, wounds, and brokenness of your circumstances. Just as soon as that is considered, open your heart and mind to this phrase: "But God . . ." Watch how He moves to heal, restore, and resurrect!

#5

Jesus loves you to bits. He died 2,000 years ago and then rose again for the honor and privilege of loving you.

#6

Juxtaposition. I love this word! Makes you think that several realities can claim the same space. Like cheered as a king and crucified as a criminal. Buried, with the slightest fragrance of a coming resurrection. It might be Friday, but Sunday is on its way!

#7

Freedom is a wonderous substance that has immeasurable worth. Someone always foots the bill, costing the payee dearly. Think about the purpose of Memorial Day, our federal holiday that is acknowledged the last Monday in May. Three appropriate responses when we realize this freedom is ours: gratitude, enjoyment, and utilization!

#8

You might hear Father's voice with crystal clarity. You might execute His request with exacting precision. You might sit back to watch for a victory that doesn't manifest. You ask, "Father, what do I get for hearing Your voice and obeying, if it is not victory?" He might laugh and answer, "Oh, that is easy! You get another battle!" If you are a true warrior, another battle will make your heart leap for joy! "Do not grow weary in well doing!" (Galatians 6:9).

#9

Sometimes, the mountain you move with your miniscule faith is not the one you intended. However, watching mountains move is breathtaking. Sometimes, the miracle you are gifted is not the one for which you prayed. Nevertheless, your heart will be just as full. Life is a curious thing!

#10

Just like physical wounds heal and form a scar, our emotional wounds can do the same thing. Scars do not hurt! They document a moment in time. Emotionally, if we choose to do the work, we can walk in joy and peace despite tragic and traumatic times. When you release your pain to God, you receive back His healing. It manifests as life, joy, peace, goodness, love, generosity, and self-love.

#11

So many things I don't know. That list of things has gotten longer as I have aged. This I do know: Christ was crucified and then raised from the dead. Honestly, these two facts impact my life every minute. Forgiveness and the power to overcome cannot be quantified, neither should they be underestimated.

#12

Stress is the world's way of saying, "You're not adequate." Peace is God's way of saying, "I AM."[4]

#13

Does today find you anxious, lonely, or sad? Does today find you battling illness, depression, or failure? Does today find you happy, prospering, or whole? Bring it to the cross. Bring it all to the cross. This life, though significant, is fleeting in the face of eternity. That blood that was shed on Calvary was shed for you. Its power is available every day to touch you where you really are. I speak, "Comfort, Strength, and Healing." I speak, "Joy, Hope, and Love."

#14

It's time for a real gut check. No pointing fingers. Take a good look in the mirror and decide to come up higher. Repentance is a word rarely heard in our churches, much less our culture. But now is the time for us to turn from our individual destructive ways. Yes, I'm talking to myself. Here is a "Me Too" that I wish would go viral.

Chapter 5

Relationships

#1

As much as you are able, notice the good in people and articulate it. Tell them. Tell their child or friend. Use your words to bless and encourage. We are all in transformational times. Everyone could use a few accolades by being told what they are doing correctly.

#2

Two things we can always improve on:

1. Love people where they are, not where you wish they were.

2. Listen to what people are actually saying, not what you think they are saying.

#3

Put some time in your schedule for shenanigans and making people smile. Laughter does good like medicine. (Proverbs 17:22)

#4

Let go of the liars, cheaters, and manipulators. The only one qualified to legitimately pass judgment on you, Who was sinless, chose instead to love the snot out of you! He made a way to snatch every pain and transgression and replace them with peace through friendship.

#5

We need love as much as we need air. If you have the chance to extend a kindness, an encouragement, or a smile, if you have the chance to be generous, or helpful, or selfless, just do it. Do something, no matter how small, to help someone besides yourself. The world contains many selfish, self-centered people. Let's ignore that and fill the world with love.

#6

I am sorry you were betrayed, lied about, abused, or abandoned. I'm sorry if your parents were absent or narcissists. You weren't supposed to be treated that way. No one is supposed to be treated that way. I pray that this is the year where we allow God to heal our emotional wounds. I pray that you come to know and deeply embrace the reality that you are a dream come true from His very being. Your value is indescribable and immeasurable. You were bought at a price—the precious blood of Christ. He can save us to the utmost. Let's stoke the flames of revival and watch Him pour out His power and His presence.

#7

Everyone you meet today could use a good chuckle, a kind word, or encouragement. If they are in the middle of a crisis, they might also need a shoulder to cry on. Today is a good day to be the change you want to see in the world.

#8

Every day, we are surrounded by packages labeled "Offense." As much as possible, walk on by. Refuse to pick them up! Remember, a kind word turns away wrath (Proverbs 15:1). Bear in mind, even a fool is thought wise when he is silent (Proverbs 17:28).

#9

In a world that can be trying and tumultuous, be a class act.

#10

When you are struggling and someone makes things all the harder, that is not love. If people in your life habitually make everything difficult because of their drama, let them go!

#11

In every corner of your city, people need this: kindness, caring, understanding, and patience. They need someone to listen to them. They need someone to encourage them. Those things cost zero dollars. They are free for the giving and taking. In trying times, we need to get back to basics: Love one another (John 13:34).

#12

You cannot do the ordinary and expect extraordinary results. Be a trailblazer. Character counts. At the end of your days, two things remain behind: your character, and your relationships.

#13

Don't bring a wishbone to an occasion requiring a backbone. One is used daily, the other only once after eating a chicken or a turkey.

Chapter 6

Value

#1

Two things, of many, that money cannot buy: peace of mind and joy.

#2

Aim high. Dig deep. You are already loved, adored, accepted, and provided for. How much are you worth? Value is calculated by how much someone is willing to pay for something. Everything was given for you. Nothing was held back. Everything was poured out. Your worth is incalculable.

#3

Believe in the impossible. Get creative in the ways you care about the people in your circle. Think kind and grace-filled thoughts about yourself. Your worth and value are beyond description. You are simply priceless.

#4

Since there are so many messages to the contrary that come from so many directions, I just want to say, "You are good enough! You are actually amazing!"

Chapter 7

Forgiveness

#1

If you as much as whisper softly, "I am sorry," God takes your mess up and obliterates it. He doesn't store it or catalog it. He looks at His account book, and all He sees is a dazzling white page.

#2

If God, in His wisdom, has removed your transgression, then the next order of business is to receive that gift of forgiveness. If you beat yourself up over something God has removed, you are saying His system of grace is not good enough.

#3

If God has placed your offense at the bottom of the Sea of Forgetfulness, please do not purchase fishing gear and bring it back to the surface. Choose to allow God to be the garbage man and remove it forever. Allow that relief and freedom from the stench and residue of sin to fill you with newness of life! Remember, no fishing in the Sea of Forgetfulness.

#4

How far is the East from the West? Infinitely separated. Your forgiven sin only exists in the minds that choose to remember. If you ask God about something He has pardoned, His response will be, "I apologize, I don't understand what you are referring to."

#5

They may never formulate the words, "I am sorry," but you can forgive them anyway. If you are a believer, you are obligated to do just that. It is based on the fact that God forgave you, and you didn't deserve it either.

#6

No, it is not easy to forgive. It is a supernatural exchange. I can't do it without total reliance on God. My prayers start with, "Father, help me forgive."

#7

If you are a believer, forgiveness is not a side item of a salad bar. It is the centerpiece of everything we embrace. It is hard work to choose to forgive. It takes time and effort and dying to ourselves. However, what better way to represent the Christ of Christmas than to keep our hearts kind and tender towards everyone we encounter.

#8

Offering and receiving forgiveness are such supernatural transactions. "Blessed are the peacemakers, for they will be called children of God" (Matthew 5:9). "In a disagreement, what if God is more interested in reconciliation than He is about who wins the argument? What if making your point is not the point?" [5]

Chapter 8

Hope

#1

"It's a new day! Baby, it's a new day" [6.] Whatever you are facing, don't give up. Give all the pain, stress, sickness, and disappointment to The One Who gave it all for you. Lay that stuff at His feet, and in exchange, He will give comfort, peace, healing, and hope.

Father, Your kingdom has come. Your will is being done on Earth just like in Heaven. Now restore, strengthen, and transform Your people. In Jesus' name, I pray.

#2

Don't lose your grip on hope. I know many are pressing through various difficulties. Remember, the wine press produces wine, the olive press produces olive oil, and heat and pressure turn coal into diamonds!

#3

There is beauty and power in the ordinary things we experience day after day. Look for them and savor them. Fill your heart to overflowing. Always remember: Love God, love yourself, and love your neighbor.

#4

Whatever you have lost or are suffering through, He is there in the midst. Heaven is for real, and so is grief. He is catching tears, caressing your heart, and carrying you when needed. You are loved in profound, mind-boggling ways.

#5

You might feel upside down and backwards. You might feel squeezed in on every side. But in reality, you could be on the precipice of something powerfully transforming.

#6

"You're wonderful. You're beautiful. You're fantastic. That's our girl. She's more valuable than the whole planet. He can create worlds that are still being created. You have more worth than that. For every tear, you'll have a smile. For every pain, you'll have joy. With all the ashes, He is transforming your life. From this point forward you will have more joy in your salvation than you have ever had before. It will be you and Him and love." [7]

#7

If you feel like the walls around you are crumbling, take heart. Be strong and courageous. "The Crumbling brings us back to foundation. Foundation means that we're going to be rebuilding." [8]

#8

Remember, there are blooms even in the desert.

#9

Where there is a seed of hope, water that thing. Regardless of circumstance, we have worth, value, and destiny. The only person that can hold you back is you! Be bold in love, be generous, and speak words of hope and healing.

#10

"Let us run with endurance the race God has set before us."
(Hebrews 12:1)

The use of the word "endurance" suggests two things:

1. The path is not easy.
2. God has provided the necessary power to make it through.

#11

God is using all the circumstances of your life—good, bad, painful, or joyful—to write His name on your heart. His love for you is beyond belief.

#12

Every difficulty, disappointment and trouble can be used as a setup for yet another triumph.

#13

Stay in the struggle. Don't quit. Hope does not disappoint us. (Romans 5:5) The unseen realm is more real than what we see and touch. Angels are being released. The factors are real, but so is the coming victory. Hang in there.

#14

A well-trained runner will jump over every hurdle. They do not stop at the barrier and describe it. They pay it no attention other than the force necessary to conquer it. Do not be distracted by the crowd, the statistics, nor the obstacles. Keep your focus forward. Run your race with endurance.

#15

In the frustration, I speak, "Endurance." In the pain, I speak, "Comfort." In the chaos, I speak, "Silence." In the darkness, I speak, "Light." Unprecedented times yield unprecedented insights and strengths. Bless you, friends. None of this is easy, but there is the other side.

Chapter 9

Prayer

#1

Don't ever be intimidated to pray. There are no atheists in fox holes. Simply talk to Him as you would a friend.

#2

In everything you face, be strong and exceedingly courageous, and make your appeal to Heaven.

#3

"Help!" That is one power-packed utterance when directed at the King of Kings and Lord of Lords. When the Creator of the cosmos hears that distress signal emanating out of one of His sons or daughters, He will answer. He might calm your anxious heart or give you a brilliant idea. Either way, He is with you in your chaos. Pray it as often as necessary.

#4

I heard what the doctors said. I did! My question is this, "What do You say, God? What do You say about all of this?"

I don't know how many hundreds of times I prayed this for Carly. I don't know how many thousands of times I have prayed just that last part, but it is one of my favorite prayers to pray.

#5

Carly's birth was a fifteen-hour marathon. The OBGYN's last words before the C-section were, "You are only going to have time to bond and say goodbye." As her cries pierced the air of the delivery room, I wept. Waves of love, gratitude, and relief overwhelmed my fatigued body. I believe in miracles even on difficult days.

#6

A simple prayer for salvation:

> *Father, thank You for prompting my heart today to be reconciled with You. I believe that You forgive mistakes, transgressions, and willful disobedience. I give You all my sins. Wash me, and I will be whiter than snow. (Psalms 51:7) I need You in my life. I need Your guidance. I want Your friendship. I recognize You as my Savior. Now come into my life and lead me from this day forward.*

#7

A prayer of repentance for my city:

> *Father, forgive us, for we don't know what we do. Forgive us for allowing petty things to fill our lives. Forgive us for the microscopes we hold to examine each other's specks; all the while our logs remain. Forgive us for allowing lawless things like bitterness, abortion, immorality, discrimination, and sex trafficking to advance here. Forgive us for our many idols. Father, pour out Your holiness into our churches so we will repent. Father, send Your revival in any form and through anyone You choose, even our children. In Jesus' name I pray.*

Chapter 10

Not Far from Here

*W*e are cleaning my car at the local Gate Express Carwash. However, our ultimate destination is Mayo Clinic. As we drive, I notice a sunbeam coming through one particular cirrus cloud. This is not the kind of weather that will result in a rainstorm or any kind of driving difficulty. The puffy clouds are everywhere. I long to comprehensively soak in the evening sky, to recognize nuances and movements. I pretend plan a future date to take an entire day to observe the heavens and photograph them.

But not far from here someone is dying. Not far from here, someone is crying with the pieces of a broken heart. Not far from here, babies are being born, families are rejoicing, and couples are saying, "I do."

This world is wonderful and wild and breathtaking all in one fell swoop. I scratch my head. I fall to my knees. I rejoice and practice being grateful. I plead for friends in the unseen realm of the Courts of Heaven. I expect to see God move and simultaneously, am grateful that this world is home for just a microsecond considering the longevity of this time frame: eternity.

I watch the nurses and doctor intently work through a lingering crisis. I talk to Andre's beautiful daughter. We sing when it is appropriate. We pray. We encourage. We hope.

I pull from my experience as a cryptologic technician, and I try to comprehend when Andre speaks. I pull my hair back and lean to strain for audible words. I catch a word here and there.

Apart from this current circumstance, Andre is a mighty man of love, joy and integrity. His greatest wish is that all would come to know his Savior, Jesus. He would tell you that there is nothing you have ever done that would cause God to lose hope in your future. He would tell you of a cross and an empty tomb. That we have all fallen short through our own choices, but God, being the Creator of the entire cosmos, made a way for a deep friendship with Him.

There was a long time in history that only the High Priest would enter into the Holy of Holies (His Presence), and atone for the sins of the nation once a year. Now, with the perfect blood of Jesus having been brought to the mercy seat, there is nothing in the way of a restoration. We can live in communion with Him. His presence belongs to all of the Beloved.

Not far from here, someone just found out about their soon coming promotion. Someone else is filling a U-haul that will rearrange living conditions and holidays, ad nauseam.

In all the shifting sand, and varied times, I hope you find a safe place to stand. I hope you establish your life on the firm foundation of our Resurrected King.

"So everyone who hears these words of Mine and acts upon them [obeying them] will be like a sensible (prudent, practical, wise) man who built his house upon the rock. And the rain fell and the floods came and the winds blew and beat against that house; yet it did not fall, because it had been founded on the rock." Matthew 7:24-25 AMPC

Chapter 11

Timeless Treasure

The Lord's Prayer

Matthew 6:9-13

Our Father, Who art in Heaven
hallowed be Thy Name

Thy Kingdom come,
Thy Will be done,
on earth as it is in Heaven.

Give us this day our daily bread.
And forgive us our trespasses,
as we forgive those that trespass against us.

And lead us not into temptation,
but deliver us from evil

For Thine is the Kingdom,
and the power, and the glory,
forever and ever. Amen

The Ten Commandments

Exodus 20:2-17

- I am the LORD your God who brought you out of the land of Egypt, out of the house of bondage. You shall have no other gods before Me
- You shall not make for yourself a carved image—any likeness of anything that is in heaven above, or that is in the earth beneath, or that is in the water under the earth; you shall not bow down to them nor serve them. For I, the LORD your God, am a jealous God, visiting the iniquity of the fathers upon the children to the third and fourth generations of those who hate Me, but showing mercy to thousands, to those who love Me and keep My commandments
- You shall not take the name of the LORD your God in vain, for the LORD will not hold him guiltless who takes His name in vain.
- Observe the Sabbath day, to keep it holy, as the LORD your God commanded you. Six days you shall labor and do all your work, but the seventh day is the Sabbath of

the LORD your God. In it you shall do no work: you, nor your son, nor your daughter, nor your male servant, nor your female servant, nor your ox, nor your donkey, nor any of your cattle, nor your stranger who is within your gates, that your male servant and your female servant may rest as well as you. And remember that you were a slave in the land of Egypt, and the LORD your God brought you out from there by a mighty hand and by an outstretched arm; therefore the LORD your God commanded you to keep the Sabbath day.

- Honor your father and your mother, as the LORD your God has commanded you, that your days may be long, and that it may be well with you in the land which the LORD your God is giving you.
- You shall not murder
- You shall not commit adultery
- You shall not steal
- You shall not bear false witness against your neighbor
- You shall not covet your neighbor's wife; and you shall not desire your neighbor's house, his field, his male servant, his female servant, his ox, his donkey, or anything that is your neighbor's

FATHER'S LOVE LETTER[9]

FATHER'S LOVE LETTER
An intimate message from God to you.

My Child,

You may not know me, but I know everything about you. Psalm 139:1 I know when you sit down and when you rise up. Psalm 139:2 I am familiar with all your ways. Psalm 139:3 Even the very hairs on your head are numbered. Matthew 10:29-31 For you were made in my image. Genesis 1:27 In me you live and move and have your being. Acts 17:28 For you are my offspring. Acts 17:28 I knew you even before you were conceived. Jeremiah 1:4-5 I chose you when I planned creation. Ephesians 1:11-12 You were not a mistake, for all your days are written in my book. Psalm 139:15-16 I determined the exact time of your birth and where you would live. Acts 17:26 You are fearfully and wonderfully made. Psalm 139:14 I knit you together in your mother's womb. Psalm 139:13 And brought you forth on the day you were born. Psalm 71:6 I have been misrepresented by those who don't know me. John 8:41-44 I am not distant and angry, but am the complete expression of love. 1 John 4:16 And it is my desire to lavish my love on you. 1 John 3:1 Simply because you are my child and I am your Father. 1 John 3:1 I offer you more than your earthly father ever could. Matthew 7:11 For I am the perfect father. Matthew 5:48 Every good gift that you receive comes from my hand. James 1:17 For I am your provider and I meet all your needs. Matthew 6:31-33 My plan for your future has always been filled with hope. Jeremiah 29:11 Because I love you with an everlasting love. Jeremiah 31:3 My thoughts toward you are countless as the sand on the seashore. Psalm 139:17-18 And I rejoice over you with singing. Zephaniah 3:17 I will never stop doing good to you. Jeremiah 32:40 For you are my treasured possession. Exodus 19:5 I desire to establish you with all my heart and all my soul. Jeremiah 32:41 And I want to show you great and marvelous things. Jeremiah 33:3 If you seek me with all your heart, you will find me. Deuteronomy 4:29 Delight in me and I will give you the desires of your heart. Psalm 37:4 For it is I who gave you those desires. Philippians 2:13 I am able to do more for you than you could possibly imagine. Ephesians 3:20 For I am your greatest encourager. 2 Thessalonians 2:16-17 I am also the Father who comforts you in all your troubles. 2 Corinthians 1:3-4 When you are brokenhearted, I am close to you. Psalm 34:18 As a shepherd carries a lamb, I have carried you close to my heart. Isaiah 40:11 One day I will wipe away every tear from your eyes. Revelation 21:3-4 And I'll take away all the pain you have suffered on this earth. Revelation 21:3-4 I am your Father, and I love you even as I love my son, Jesus. John 17:23 For in Jesus, my love for you is revealed. John 17:26 He is the exact representation of my being. Hebrews 1:3 He came to demonstrate that I am for you, not against you. Romans 8:31 And to tell you that I am not counting your sins. 2 Corinthians 5:18-19 Jesus died so that you and I could be reconciled. 2 Corinthians 5:18-19 His death was the ultimate expression of my love for you. 1 John 4:10 I gave up everything I loved that I might gain your love. Romans 8:31-32 If you receive the gift of my son Jesus, you receive me. 1 John 2:23 And nothing will ever separate you from my love again. Romans 8:38-39 Come home and I'll throw the biggest party heaven has ever seen. Luke 15:7 I have always been Father, and will always be Father. Ephesians 3:14-15 My question is... Will you be my child? John 1:12-13 I am waiting for you. Luke 15:11-32

Love, Your Dad
Almighty God

Personal Thoughts and Reflections

_____

_____

_____

_____

_____

_____

_____

_____

_____

_____

_____

_____

_____

_____

_____

_____

_____

_____

_____

Endnotes

Chapter 1

1 Minnesota Dept of Health, Information about Trisomy 18, January 4, 2024, www.health.state.mn.us/diseases/cy/trisomy18.html

Chapter 2

2 Unknown, Facebook Post, January 10, 2021, shorturl.at/Lcc5D

3 Unknown, Facebook Post, August 10, 2021, shorturl.at/O0wy9

Chapter 4

4 Dean Lewis, direct message to author, July 19, 2021

Chapter 7

5 Pastor Jerry Sweat, Facebook Post, June 8, 2020, shorturl.at/oQbIm

Chapter 8

6 Johnny Seay Band, New Day 1984, Google.com/search?q=Johnny+Seay+Band%2C+New+day+1984

7 Paul Michelle, Facebook Post, February 28, 2021, shorturl.at/VuRjw

8 Pastor Tracy Perez, Facebook response to a post by Deborah Lewis, May 5, 2021, shorturl.at/LqnNA

Chapter 11

9 Father's Love letter, © 1999 Father Heart Communications, Fathersloveletter.com/text.html

Printed in the USA
CPSIA information can be obtained
at www.ICGtesting.com
LVHW050845210824
788785LV00012B/238

9 798868 500770